This book is dedicated to Aline and William

The author of this book Benjamin James Baillie
lives and works in Normandy

THE NORMAN CRUSADE

The First Crusade and the Conquest of the Kingdom of Heaven

1095 – 1099 AD

By Benjamin James Baillie

Contents

Bohemond De Hauteville
"Prince of Antioch"

Introduction

Christianity's counterattack had started long before the First Crusade in 1095. Three centuries had passed since Charles Martel had halted the Muslim invasion of Europe at the battle of Poitiers in 736 AD. By the 11th century the Christians were on the offensive. The legendary El Cid had started the fight back against the Moors in the Iberian Peninsula and just before the turn of the century the Normans under the De Hauteville brothers had conquered the Muslim stronghold of Sicily; further reading in my book "**THE FIRST MAFIA**" **The Norman Conquest of Southern Italy and Sicily**. In 1071 Seljuk Turks captured the Holy city of Jerusalem from the more tolerant Fatimid Muslims and by 1076 they had all but closed off the city and Holy land to pilgrims. In 1095 the call to arms by Pope Urban II would lead to the First Crusade and embitter Christian and Muslim relations for centuries to come and still have consequences to this very day.

The call to arms

In 1095 ambassadors from the Byzantine Emperor Alexius arrived at the Papal court asking for help against the Seljuk Turks who had conquered most of Byzantine Anatolia (Turkey).The Emperor hoped that with western military support he would be able to regain Byzantine territory lost to the Turks.

Clermont Ferrand 1095

"He, who welcomes to me, let him deny himself, take up his cross and follow me".

In November 1095 the Council of Clermont gathered in the medieval city of Clermont Ferrand (France). Pope Urban II gave a rousing speech to the people. He called upon all of Christendom to take up arms and liberate the Holy land from the Muslims. The crowd and clergy responded with the Crusader chant: **"DIEU LI VOLT" (God wills it!)**
The Pope offered anyone who went on Crusade absolution from sin and it was firmly believed at the time that participating in the Crusade was an act of the highest good.

The Pope's agenda was not just a spiritual belief in the ideals of Crusade, but also a chance to pull into line the Heretic church of the Eastern Roman Empire (The Byzantine Empire) and to cement Papal Supremacy over the Kings, Emperor and Princes of Europe.

The Council of Clermont, November 1095

After the Pope's speech the idea of Crusade spread around Europe like wildfire. Old and young, noble and poor were galvanized into action. In an age where the power of religion was far more important to people than in the present day the Crusade offered the opportunity to guarantee a place in Heaven

The 3000 mile journey

The first Crusaders to make the 3000 thousand mile journey were badly organized. Peter the Hermit led a fanatical peasant army across Europe causing widespread damage in Hungary before they reached Constantinople in the summer in 1096. While Peter stayed in Constantinople many of his followers continued into the hostile lands of the Seljuk Turks. It was a disaster, with no central command the small Crusader groups were massacred by their Seljuk foes.

The gathering of the Titans

In August 1096 the main Crusader armies set off for the Byzantine capital of Constantinople. Some of the most famous and richest warriors of the age made up the major contingents. From the Anglo-Norman world came Robert Duke of Normandy (son of William the Conqueror), Bohemond De Hauteville (son of Robert Guiscard) Tancred his nephew, Rainulf son of William "Iron arm" and other members of the De Hauteville family led the Italian-Normans.

From France came Raymond Count of Toulouse who had already fought against the Muslim Moors in Spain, Godfrey of Bouillon, Robert Count of Flanders, Stephen Count of Blois, Baldwin, Godfrey and Eustace III of Boulogne and Adhemar Bishop of Le Puy.

Robert Duke of Normandy (Gloucester Cathedral)

Constantinople 1096-1097

By the spring of 1097 all the major contingents had arrived in Constantinople. For the Byzantine Emperor Alexius this was not what he had envisaged, instead of the Western mercenaries that he had hoped for he now had thousands of zealous Crusaders in and around his capital.

He was extremely suspicious of the motives of some of the Crusader commanders, especially Bohemond De Hauteville whom he had previously fought before during the wars against Robert Guiscard and the Normans. The Emperor's daughter Anna Comnena commented:

"Bohemond is psychically strong, brave and has an unruly wild temper. He is the exact stamp of his father Robert Guiscard, and is a living model of his father's character. During their war against us in the Balkans they were nicknamed the Caterpillar and the Locust. For whatever escaped Robert, his son Bohemond grabbed and destroyed"

Alexius demanded that the Crusader commanders swear an oath of allegiance unto him and that any former Byzantine land conquered during the campaign should be returned to the Empire. Some of the Normans refused to swear allegiance. Tancred and Richard of the Participate escaped from the city and rejoined the Crusader army on the other side of the Bosporus.

The attack on Nicaea 1097

Nicaea was the first major Muslim city that stood in the way of the Crusader march to the Holy land. The capital of the Sultanate of Rum would have to be captured to avoid the supply lines being cut or being attacked from behind. On the 6th of May 1097 the Crusader forces of Robert de Normandy, and Stephen de Blois surrounded the city and began the siege. When the other contingents arrived the besieging force swelled to over forty five thousand professional troops. A further 3000 Byzantine troops sent by Alexuis under the command Tatikois and Tzitas.

A Turkish relief force tried to break through but were held at bay by the troops of Raymond de Toulouse and then annihilated when the Count of Flanders men smashed into their flank. After a month of siege the city surrendered not to the besiegers, but to the Byzantines. At the same time as the negotiations were taking place the Crusaders were scaling the city walls.

The gates opened only to reveal the Byzantine Imperial banner flying from the citadel.

It was a huge disappointment, the Crusaders wanted to sack the city and receive the spoils of war.

They were even more galled when the Turkish garrison received safe conduct from the Byzantines.

The Ancient walls of Nicaea

The battle of Dorylaeum from a lost stain glass window St Denis, Paris

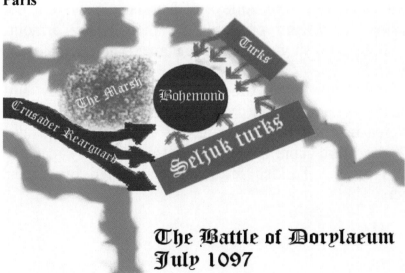

The Battle of Dorylaeum
July 1097

The Battle of Dorlaeum

The army marched off into the hostile interior of Asia Minor led by the Byzantines then followed by the Normans of Bohemond and Robert of Normandy. In late June the Norman scouts returned to the column and announced that the Turks were preparing for battle. Bohemond ordered the Crusaders to form up into a defensive position near a swamp until the second contingent of Crusaders arrived.

The Turkish cavalry unleashed a deadly barrage of arrows and spears at the Crusaders. This was the first time the westerners had been subjected to such harrying tactics. They were completely shocked by this new form of warfare and fled towards their defensive camp. Robert Duke of Normandy rallied the men by lifting up his helmet, and Shouting **"NORMANDIE, NORMANDIE"**, Just as his father had done before him at the Battle of Hastings in 1066. Confined to a defensive position they held off the Turkish attacks for over 7 hours. The sky turned black from the volleys of Turkish arrows but the Crusaders held firm protected by their heavy armour. Indeed the Turkish gave them the name "The Iron people" afterwards.

Reinforcements from Adhemar Bishop of Le Puy and Godfrey of Bouillon arrived in the nick of time and bolstered up the Crusaders ranks. Both sides fought hard until the third contingent of Crusader heavy cavalry arrived on the Turkish left and steamrolled over their archers.

Robert Duke of Normandy (The Battle of Dorylaeum 1097)

Bohemond said **"if it pleases God today, you will all become rich"** the Christians rallied and afterwards ransacked the Sultans camp. Victory was complete and although it had been a shaky start the Crusaders were convinced that God was on their side and they were invincible.

After the defeat at Dorylaeum Sultan Kilij Arslan I withdrew from the region and left the Crusaders to march on virtually unmolested. The local Christian and Greek communities of the cities and towns opened their gates and welcomed the Crusaders as liberators.

The Battle of Dorlaeum

The Crusade splits

The Crusaders had forefilled their part of the bargain with the Byzantine Emperor Alexius by recovering most of Anatolia for him. So far as the Crusaders were concerned it had been a one sided deal. They had done all the hard work for little reward. Indeed some members of the Crusade were now thinking about carving out a Kingdom for themselves. On the Roman road outside Heraclea a Turkish host hoped to ambush the Crusaders. It was routed by Bohemond and the Normans in the advanced guard. They marched into the Tarus Mountains and at the Cilican gates Tancred De Hauteville and Baldwin De Boulogne split from the main force and headed south into Cilicia and northern Syria.

Land grabbing

It is probably certain that both men intended to secure fiefs for themselves. Baldwin's wife had died on the long march after the battle of Dorylaeum and with her any reason he had for returning to France. Tancred may have all along used the excuse of the Crusade to further his designs on a new Norman State in the east. They both laid siege to Tarsus then Tancred spurred on and captured Adana and Mamistra. The two hot headed commanders nearly came to blows at Mamistra. Tancred headed south towards Antioch. Baldwin received a curious offer from Thoros of Edessa who offered him the chance to become the Lord of the County of Edessa when he died in exchange for the military muscle of Baldwin's Crusaders. In March 1098 Thoros was assassinated and Baldwin was proclaimed Lord of Edessa. He established the first Latin Crusader state in the Holy land.

Baldwin, the first Crusader lord of Edessa 1098

The siege of Antioch

In October 1097 the main Crusader army reached Antioch. Antioch is situated on one of the great trade routes between east and west and was one of the most important cities in the Middle East since its foundation by Alexander the Great. When the vast Crusader army came into view Yaghi Siyan (the Turkish Governor) sent out ambassadors to every corner of the Muslim world requesting urgent help and assistance. Raymond De Toulouse wanted to the attack the city immediately but Bohemond urged caution and suggested a siege. Indeed the mighty Byzantine built walls around Antioch were virtually impregnable.

Stephen De Blois stated:
"We found before us the city of Antioch. It is very large and fortified, with the greatest strength and almost impossible to be taken by force alone".

The Crusaders encircled the city and began the siege. Antioch would be their greatest test of faith to date. If they were to fail here there would be no going back.

Each Crusader contingent blocked off access to the main five gatehouses of the city.

The walls of Antioch

The coastal port of Latakia was captured by an Anglo-Saxon fleet in the service of the Byzantines. These warriors were probably refugees from England after the Norman Conquest and were led by Edgar the Atheling (the Anglo Saxon heir to the throne of England). Without the supplies brought in from the captured ports the Crusader siege around Antioch would have failed. As the Siege dragged on throughout the winter conditions became terrible.

Stephen De Blois wrote;

"Throughout the whole winter we suffered from excessive cold and enormous torrents of rain. What some say about the impossibility of bearing the heat of the sun in Syria is untrue, for the winter here is very similar to our winter in the West."

With supplies dangerously low and the extreme cold effecting Crusader moral Bohemond and Robert of Flanders set out with 20,000 men raiding the neighboring districts for food. At the same time Duqaq of Damascus was leading a Muslim relief army towards Antioch.

The Battle of Harenc December 1097

Duqaq's scouts returned to him and reported that the Crusader army was close and unaware of their presence. At once Duqaq ordered a forced march and attacked Robert of Flanders division. The Saracens came into view and quickly overwhelmed and surrounded Roberts force.
Desperate hand to hand fighting ensued. Robert's men were on the verge of complete annihilation when Bohemond who was also in the vicinity saw the swirling clouds of dust in the distance and realized what was happening.
He spurred his horse and ordered a direct cavalry charge. The Saracens were now enveloped by Bohemond's Norman Crusaders. It was pure carnage; the Crusaders from inside the envelopment fought their way out as Bohemond's troops rode down the Saracens trying to escape. The remnants of the Damascene army retreated and had to abandon their attempt to relieve Antioch.
Although the Crusaders had again won a great victory, the area was too dangerous to continue foraging. They returned triumphant to Antioch but also empty handed.

Antioch December 1097

When Yaghi Siyan saw that Bohemond and Robert of Flanders troops had withdrawn from Antioch he decided to try and defeat the remaining Crusaders who surrounded the city.

In a daring nighttime raid the city's garrison attacked the main Crusader camp. Although initially surprised by the assault, the Crusaders rallied and Raymond de Toulouse's men forced the Turks to retreat back into Antioch.

The Siege of Antioch

1098

The siege continued into the New Year. Both sides were suffering from hunger and the weather. On a cold February night Peter the Hermit one of the Crusades most ardent religious followers attempted to leave the siege. Fearing a general collapse of nerve and moral if he escaped, Bohemond ordered Tancred to capture him and bring him back to camp. Tancred forced Peter to return under pain of death, thus avoiding the crisis.

The second battle outside Antioch

The Crusaders got wind of another Saracen plan to relieve Antioch. This time Ridwan, Lord of Aleppo was marching towards the city with a huge army. Bohemond was chosen to lead the remaining 700 armoured knights into battle.

Indeed Bohemond may have used his childhood knowledge of guerilla warfare in Sicily from his father Robert Guiscard and Uncle Count Roger to defeat the Saracens. As although outnumbered he would use the terrain to defeat them.

Near the Iron Bridge Bohemond sent a detachment of knights to attack the Turks. The knights charged in and then conducted a feinted retreat. The Turks who thought they were retreating chased after them. Not realizing that they were been being drawn into a trap; it was too late, with the river Orontes on their left and the lake on their right. The area was unsuitable for them to use their vast numbers.

At the last moment Bohemond led the Crusader heavy cavalry directly into the ranks of the surprised Turks. They simply rode down everything in their path. Bohemond hacked down man and horse. The Christian knights were in frenzy, covered from head to toe in the blood of their enemies. Victory was complete and the legend of the Crusader heavy cavalry now spread throughout the Muslim world.

Crusaders against their Saracen foes

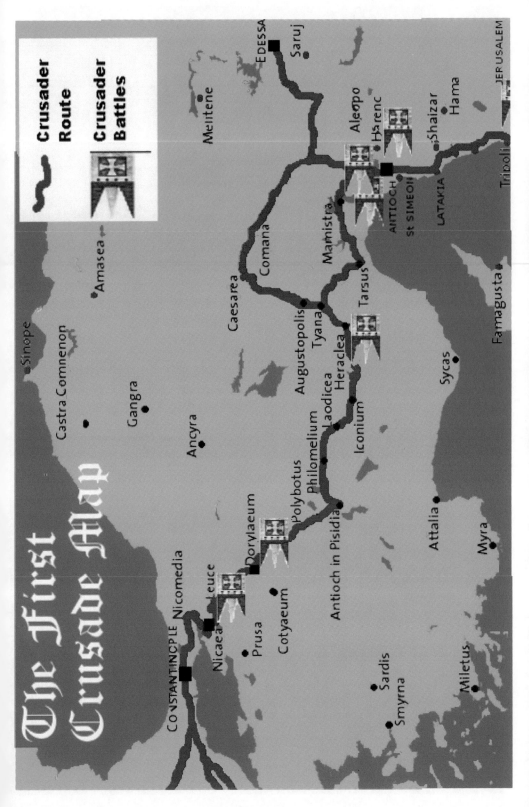

Spring 1098

In the spring of 1098 spies brought disturbing information to the Crusader commanders. Kerbogha of Mosul was raising an almighty army of over 75.000 men to destroy the Christian besiegers. The Crusades leaders discussed the situation. Bohemond suggested that Antioch should be given to whoever could take it and once captured it should not be handed over to the Byzantines. Since the Byzantine representative Taticius had left the siege the leaders saw no reason why Antioch should be handed back. After all they had suffered throughout the siege with little help from the Emperor Alexius. By May 1098 Kerbogha's army fell upon the fledgling Crusader state of Edessa. The Saracen army laid siege to Baldwin's hilltop fortress but was unable to budge him from his defensive position. After a month of futile besieging Kerbogha gave up and headed off to confront the Crusaders at Antioch.

Antioch Captured

Meanwhile Bohemond had entered into secret negotiations with Firouz, one of Antioch's castellans, to hand over the city to him. After over eight months of terrible conditions and destroying two armies sent against them, the Crusaders moment had come.

On the 2nd of June Stephen de Blois left Antioch fearing he would be killed by the approaching Saracen army. The rest of the Crusaders pretended to leave the siege and marched off to confront Kerbogha. In reality they secretly returned during the evening. Bohemond's Normans assembled beneath the tower of the Two Sisters. Firouz gave the signal from the battlements. Fulk de Chartres climbed a ladder along with a party of 60 Knights and entered Antioch. They crept along the city walls, dispatched the guards and with the help of some Christian inhabitants opened the mighty St George gate. The main army who were waiting outside stormed into the city. Shouting their war cry **"GOD WILL'S IT!"** the Crusaders went on the rampage, ransacking and massacring the Muslim population. The streets were filled with the bodies of the slain. The frustration built up over eight months had been unleashed upon the people of the city. The slaughter of Antioch brought out all the horrors of the medieval sack. Bohemond commented; **"We wept for their wives, children and servants"**.

Crusader and Saracen battle each other during the Siege of Antioch 13th century French Manuscript

Antioch's Governor Yaghi Siyan tried to flee the city but was set upon by some Armenian peasants who pulled him from his horse and decapitated him. His head was sent back to Antioch and given to Bohemond as a present.

The remnants of the garrison held out in the citadel. Bohemond claimed the city for himself but there was little time to celebrate as Kerbogha's army was only a few miles away. Antioch was made as defensible as possible during the circumstances. More Crusaders deserted the city fearing the worst. William de Grand-Mesnil slipped out and joined up with Stephen de Blois who was heading towards the Byzantine Emperor's camp at Alexandretta. Indeed when they arrived they told the Emperor that he should return to Constantinople as all was lost at Antioch. Guy Bohemond's half-brother tried to persuade Alexuis to go on to the assistance of the Crusaders but to no avail as the Emperor decided not to risk everything in what he believed to be a lost cause.

When the news reached Antioch that there would be no assistance from the Byzantines the rank and file and many of the nobles cursed them for not having the courage to help their fellow Christians, the Crusaders were on their own.

The Discovery of the Holy Lance

Kerbogha's army surrounded Antioch and cut off any supplies from entering in and out of the city. The Crusader's moral dropped and many feared this was the end of their epic journey in the quest to retake the Holy Land from the infidel.

The mood inside changed on the 14th of June when Peter of Bartholomew a priest /pilgrim in Count Raymond's retinue, came forward and preached to the crowd that he had been visited in his dreams by St Andrew. The Saint had told him he would find the Holy Lance that had pierced Jesus inside the church of Saint Peter. Peter immediately started digging up the floor within the church. Knee deep in dirt and rock Peter started to sing and shout. The Crusader onlookers were amazed when he held high above him the relic of the Holy Lance. The discovery of the Holy Lance was seen as a good omen. With their faith renewed the Crusaders decided to take the fight to Kerbogha instead of huddling behind the walls of Antioch.

The Final battle for Antioch

On the 28th of June 1098 the Crusader army opened the Bridge gate and marched out to confront the Saracens. Adhemar Bishop of Puy commanded the Crusader left flank which was protected by the river Orontes. Bohemond led the centre with Robert Duke of Normandy. Hugh de Vermandois commanded the right wing with the last remaining cavalry. Kerbogha could not believe that the Crusaders dared attack his mighty army. He sent in the Saracen cavalry and archers who conducted a feinted flight, but when the rest of the army saw them retreating they lost heart and began in panic. Kerbogha set fire to the grassland to try and halt the Crusader advance but they saw visions of Saint George in the sky and attacked the retreating Saracen army with vigour.

Bishop Adhemar held up the Holy Lance and stated;

"Behold soldiers, St George, St Maurice, St Theodore have come to your help"

It was a slaughter with the Crusader heavy infantry cutting down everything in its way. By the time they reached the Iron Bridge the battlefield was littered with thousands of dead Muslim warriors. Kerbogha abandoned the field and returned to Mosul a broken man.

For the Crusaders it was the ultimate God given victory. Nothing could stop them now.

The final battle for Antioch June 28th 1098, Left of the picture Bishop Adhemar holds before him the Holy lance

For the remaining half of 1098 the Crusaders instead of marching on Jerusalem fought amongst themselves. Bohemond claimed Antioch and refused to give it up. He had led the Crusade from the front and won many battles against the enemies of Christendom but now he decided for him the Crusade was over. The Byzantine Emperor sent a letter to Antioch

"You know the oaths and promises which you all took in Constantinople. Now you break them by retaining Antioch and other cities. The right thing to do is to leave these cities so not to provoke more wars and trouble".

Bohemond replied;

"It is not I, but you, who are the cause of all this. For you promised you would follow us with a vast army, but you never made good your promise. When we reached Antioch we fought for months under great difficulty both against the enemy and against famine, which was more severe than had ever been experienced before, with the result that most of us ate of the very foods which are forbidden by law. We endured for a long time and while we were in this danger even Taticius, your Majesty's most loyal servant, whom you had appointed to help us, went away and left us to our danger. Yet we captured Antioch unexpectedly and utterly routed the troops which had been sent to destroy us. In what way would it be just for us to deprive ourselves willingly of what we gained by our own sweat and toil? "

Jerusalem 1098

The Fatimid Government in Egypt decided to launch their own offensive not against the Crusaders but against the Seljuk Turks who had their hands full against the Crusaders and Byzantines in Asia Minor and Syria. They retook Jerusalem from the Seljuk's without much bloodshed. Indeed the Islamic world was torn apart by division. The Fatimid regime still believed that the Crusaders were just mercenaries working for the Byzantines. If they had understood that the Westerners were intent on destroying Islam and conquering the entire Holy Land they may well have joined forces with their fellow Muslim brothers.

The Holy City of Jerusalem

The Road to Jerusalem 1099

.

In December 1098 the Crusader army attacked Maaret en Numan and sacked the city. It was one of the worst atrocities that the Crusaders had committed thus far. Man, woman, child and dog were slain in an unparalleled act of brutality. Muslim chroniclers wrote that the Crusader soldiers were so starved and hungry that they resorted to cannibalism, eating the flesh of the slain. Some of the Crusader commanders had been stalling the march on Jerusalem in order to create their own Principalities like Bohemond had done with Antioch. Many of the ordinary soldiers were fed up and decided to march on towards Jerusalem. The army swelled with the arrival of the Anglo Saxons who burned their ships and joined the Crusader march on the Holy city.

The ordeal of Peter of Bartholomew

Ever since discovering the Holy Lance at Antioch, Peter of Bartholomew had been targeted as a fraud and charlatan by various members of the Crusader army. Peter refused to admit that the whole episode had been a scam to lift Crusader moral. In April 1099 Peter decided to undertake a trail by fire to prove his innocence. The disbelievers constructed a huge fire with logs and bush wood. Peter holding the Holy lance above him walked into the fire and then came out at the other end alive. The watching crowd was in total awe. It was a miracle he had survived. Sadly he would never see the Holy city as he had been terribly burned in the fire. For nearly two weeks he clung on to life but on the 20th of April 1099 the hero of Antioch died.

The Crusaders crossed the Dog River and entered Fatimid territory for the first time. The local Fatimid rulers tried to halt the advance of the Crusader army, but nothing could stop them from reaching their goal of advancing to the Holy city. Most of the towns and villages were abandoned by their Muslim inhabitants fearing the wrath of the western Holy warriors. The garrison at Jaffa burned the fort to the ground to avoid it being used by the Crusaders. Panic ensued and the whole region was in complete terror as to what would happen next.

The advanced guard led by Tancred de Hauteville captured Bethlehem and raised the De Hauteville Banner from the tower of the Church of the nativity (the birthplace of Jesus) in early June. Three years had pasted since many of the Crusaders had taken their vows to re-conquer the Holy land. On the 7th of June 1099 the fanatical Crusader army arrived at their rendezvous with destiny. After a 3000 mile journey they had reached the Gates of Jerusalem.

Church of the Nativity, Bethlehem

The Siege of Jerusalem 1099

Jerusalem is considered the holiest city for the Christian and Jewish faiths and the second holiest place in the Muslim world. The city had been fought over many times before the Crusaders arrived in 1099. But the siege of 1099 would be remembered by the Islamic world with consequences to this very day.

The formidable mighty walls of Jerusalem

Jerusalem's governor Iftikhar al-Dawla, poisoned the wells outside the city to deny the Crusader army any fresh local water. He also expelled the remaining Christian population from the city in case of any assistance they might give towards the Crusaders. Jerusalem would have no "Third column" traitors from within who would give up the city just like what had happened at Antioch.

The Crusader army began to surround the city. Although depleted, the army was still a formidable fighting force. It consisted of about 15,000 soldiers, 2000 of which were mounted knights and thousands of followers

The First assault

Godfrey de Bouillon, the Count of Flanders and Robert Duke of Normandy besieged the City form the north side. Raymond of Toulouse camped next to the great tower of David. The Crusaders constructed a few scaling ladders with the little material they had and made their first assault on the city at the Damascus gate. The trumpets sounded and the attack on the walls began. Although they attacked with fanatical zeal it was a complete failure, after six hours of hard fighting the attack was called off. Jerusalem would be a hard nut to crack. Many believed that they would be in for a long siege similar to that of Antioch.

The Crusaders were forced to forage far and wide in search of Water and supplies. They were often ambushed by the Saracens in the dangerous passes and hills that surrounded the city. In mid June their luck changed when a Genoese fleet managed to slip through Fatimid lines and arrive in Jaffa. With the Fatimid war galleys closing the net on them their Captain decided to scuttle his ships and use the wood to construct siege machines for the attack on Jerusalem. Tancred also managed to discover a large supply of timber located in a cave just outside the city. With these extra provisions of wood the Crusaders set about constructing two mighty siege towers and extra scaling ladders ready for the final assault.

The bare footed procession

Peter Desiderius had a vision that Bishop Adhemar de Le Puy (who had died after the last battle of Antioch) had visited him in his dreams and said;

"Tell all the Princes and People that they must march bare foot around Jerusalem invoking God'. If you do this then on the ninth day the city will be captured".

On the 8th of July 1099 the entire army and its followers marched around Jerusalem. The city's garrison mocked the Crusaders, insulting them and hurling abuse towards them. It would be a gesture that the defiant garrison would live to regret. The procession arrived at the Mount of Olives where the Clergy gave sermons encouraging the moral of the Crusaders. The high ranking leaders discussed their strategy for the final assault. Tancred may have told the story of how his Grandfather Robert Guiscard devised the plan to capture the Sicilian capital Palermo. The Normans attacked one side of Palermo's walls, drawing the city's garrison to combat them. Robert led the real attack on the other side of the city, enabling him to enter the capital via deception. The plan was decided upon; the Crusaders would simultaneously launch attacks from several directions, allowing Robert of Normandy, Robert of Flanders and Tancred to launch the strongest attack.

The Crusader Siege of Jerusalem

The final assault

On the 13th of July 1099 judgment day had arrived. There was to be no going back now. All the Crusader contingents readied themselves for the final assault on the city. The night before the attack the great siege towers were moved in some cases over a mile to throw the garrison off guard. When the morning came the Saracens were astonished. The attack commenced with the Crusader stone throwing machines hurling great pieces of rock at the city walls and gates. Flaming arrows dipped in pitch, peppered the walls and houses inside the city. Hell was unleashed upon Jerusalem. The fighting continued all day and one Crusader commented that:

"It was hard to believe how great the efforts were made on both sides during that day"

On the second day the vicious fighting continued with both sides struggling to keep up the momentum. Legend has it that a lone knight began to wave his shield around on the Mount of Olives encouraging the Crusaders to continue the attack. On the 15th of July the breakthrough came. Crusader archers managed to ignite cotton bales the defenders were using on the city walls. The flames engulfed the ramparts and forced the defenders to fall back. At once the Crusaders dropped the drawbridge on one of their towers and descended upon the battlements. Lethold and Engelbert, two Flemish Knights were the first to enter, closely followed by Tancred and the Duke of Lorraine.

The Massacre of Jerusalem

As the Crusaders pilled into the city their rage became uncontrollable. They went berserk slaughtering everything within the city. The amount of blood they shed that day was incredible. An eyewitness wrote:

"Some of our men cut off the heads of our enemies; others shot them with arrows, so that they fell from the towers into the flames. Piles of heads, hands and feet were to be seen in the streets of the city". The massacre at Antioch had been vicious but Jerusalem was pure uncontrolled religious fever.

"It was necessary to pick one's way over the bodies of men and horses. But these were small matters compared to what happened at the temple of Solomon, if I tell you the truth, it will exceed your powers of belief. So let it be suffice to say this much, at least, that in the temple and porch of Solomon, men rode in blood up to their knees and bridle reins".

On the roof of the temple the Crusaders climbed up and beheaded the survivors, men women and children. The Jewish population of the city was treated no better. The main synagogue was burned to the ground with the people inside it.

Aftermath

Following the massacre of the city the bodies of the dead were removed to stop the spread of disease and some kind of order was restored. Raymond of Toulouse was offered the title of King of Jerusalem, but he refused it. It was offered to Godfrey De Bouillon who refused the title but accepted to become Advocatus Sancti Sepulchri (Advocate of the Holy Sepulchre). On the 22nd of July 1099 the Crusader Kingdom of Jerusalem was created.

Islam's response

The few Muslim survivors that managed to escape the carnage of Jerusalem spread the terror to what they had seen. Shockwaves went around the Islamic world. The Fatimid government in Egypt raised an army to crush the Crusaders. The Saracen relief force assembled in Ascalon in early August.

In Jerusalem the new Patriarch (Arnulf of Chocques) discovered a relic of the True Cross. Possibly another ploy just like the Holy Lance at Antioch, in order the raise Crusader moral. Raymond d'Aguilers circulated a story that the Saracens intended to capture all the Crusaders under 20 and mate with them, so they could create a race of superior warriors to fight for Islam. The story only encouraged the Christians to fight on to the bitter end. A last ditch diplomatic effort was sent to try and reach a compromise, but the Crusaders rejected the offer and launched a pre-emptive attack against the Fatimids.

The Battle of Ascalon

The Crusader army left Jerusalem on the 10th of August 1099. At the head of the Army was Raymond d'Aguilers carrying the Holy Lance from Antioch. He was followed by the Patriarch with the relic of the Holy cross. All the Crusaders commanders were with the army. Tancred led a surprise attack at Ramalah and captured many men and provisions. On the 11th the Crusaders caught the Fatimid army off guard and in disarray beneath the walls of Ascalon. Although outnumbered by perhaps 5/1 they decided to attack and formed up into battle array. In the centre were Tancred, Robert of Normandy and Robert of Flanders. On the left wing was Godfrey de Bouillon and on the right was Raymond of Toulouse. The battle began with a Fatimid charge. They were stopped in their tracks by the Crusader archers who let their deadly volleys of arrows rain down into the Fatimid ranks. The Crusaders now counter attacked. The battle was hard fought in the centre. Ethiopian troops fought with great courage until Godfrey de Bouillon arrived and broke deep into their ranks.

The battle turned into a rout, Raymond of Toulouse pursued the fleeing Saracens towards the coast. The Fatimid Camp was overrun by Tancred and Robert's Normans in the centre. Godfrey's men chased the remaining Fatimids to the very gates of Ascalon itself. For the Fatimids it was a disaster losing up to 10-15,000 men. The Crusaders saw it as another divine victory. During the night they camped in the former Fatimid camp expecting to give battle the next day. Instead the Fatimid army broke up and headed home. The Muslim commander Al-fdal's personal banner had been captured and was returned to Jerusalem as a trophy of war. After the battle most of the Crusader leaders forefilled their vows in Jerusalem and started returning home.

The creation of the Kingdom of Heaven

The First Crusade had now officially come to an end. Indeed for the Medieval Christian world it would go down in legend and a miraculous affair. No other Crusade after it would be as so successful. 400 hundred years of Islamic expansion had come to an end and the time of the creation of the Kingdom of Heaven had arrived. Rising up out of the ashes of the First Crusade were the fledgling Crusader states of Antioch in the North, The County of Eddessa in the east, Tripoli on the coast and the Kingdom of Jerusalem to the south.

Seljuk Turks

Armenian Cilicia

County of Edessa

Principality of Antioch

Byzantine Empire

County of Tripoli

Kingdom of Jerusalem

The Muslim World

Fatimids

The Crusader states 1100 AD

Bohemond Prince of Antioch

Most of the Crusader states were almost always on a state of alert after the end of the First Crusade in 1099. They had enemies virtually all around them. Bohemond's personal struggle against the Byzantine Empire to hold on to Antioch raged on for years. The Norman warrior tried to extent the Principality but in 1100 while coming to the assistance of an Armenian ally, his small force of 300 knights was ambushed by Danishmend Turks at the battle of Melitene. Bohemond himself was captured along with his fellow family member Richard of the Principate and held ransom by the Turks until 1103. Fearing a complete takeover either from the Byzantines or the newly rejuvenated Turks the leading magnates of Antioch offered Tancred Bohemond's nephew the regency. Tancred proved an able regent and secured the Principalities independence. Bohemond managed to raise the ransom for his release by 1103, not without difficulty from the Byzantines who were trying to lay their hands on the Norman warlord. In 1104 Bohemond decided to return to Western Europe to recruit reinforcements and settle the disputed claim of Antioch with the Pope. Tancred was again left as regent during his absence. Bohemond arrived home in Italy and began a tour of Europe recruiting an army not to attack the Saracens in the East but to wage war on his old enemy Alexius the Byzantine Emperor. The Norman warlord managed to secure the hand of the King of France's daughter. All the preparations had been made by 1107 to launch the Crusade against the Byzantines.

Continuing his Father's work 1107

The campaign against the Byzantine Empire had become a personal grudge between the Norman De Hautevilles and Alexius ever since Robert Guiscard (Bohemond's father) had attacked the Eastern Empire in the early 1080s. After receiving mass in the church of St Nicolas (Bari) Bohemond set sail for the Albanian mainland. The Norman army that invaded the Balkans was extremely large; over 30,000 men from Italy, France, Normandy and even England crossed the Adriatic that winter. The army captured Canina and then Bohemond laid siege to Durazzo for the second time in his career. Fear struck the Byzantine court except for Alexius who said;

"Let us eat now, we shall see about Bohemond afterwards".

Failing to take the city by force, the Normans began the long siege. But just like his campaign thirty years earlier the realities of warfare set in. Hemmed in by the Byzantines who held the mountain passes and cut off from supplies from Italy the offensive faltered. In the Spring Alexius arrived on the scene and negotiations started. In the end Bohemond became a vassal of Alexius and was granted: Antioch, the port of St Simeon and the other towns within the Principality of Antioch. Bohemond returned to Italy. By 1111 he was raising another army with the intention of returning to the East or maybe of attacking the Byzantines again? He died in Norman Apulia

De Hauteville Family arms

(Italy) on the 7th of March. He never achieved his dream of overthrowing the Byzantine Emperor Alexius, but his contribution towards the success of the First Crusade remains impressive.

Without his daring, guile, leadership and determination the First Crusade is likely to have failed.

Bohemond's Mausoleum Canosa, Puglia, Italy

Antioch after Bohemond

Bohemond may have sworn to become a vassal of Alexius but Tancred held the reins of power in Antioch and refused any part in the deal. With the support of the other Crusader states the Byzantines had no chance of taking back the mighty city. Tancred died in 1112 and

Bohemond's son (Bohemond II) became regent under the guidance of Roger de Salerno. Roger was another Norman who defended the Principalities rights defeating the Seljuk Turks in several battles and skirmishes. He was cut down in 1119 at the battle of the Ager Sanguinis (the Field of Blood).

Bohemond II continued the De Hauteville family trade of warfare throughout the 1120s. In 1130 he was lured into an ambush and was killed in the fighting. A horrible tale says that he was decapitated and his head with his blond hair was embalmed, placed in a silver box and sent to the Caliph as a gruesome gift. Antioch became a vassal state of the Kingdom of Jerusalem until its capture by the Baibar Muslims in 1268.

Toros Roslin wrote:

"Antioch was captured by the wicked Caliph of Egypt, many were killed and became his prisoners, all the holy temples, houses of God, which are in it were destroyed by fire." The empty title of "Prince of Antioch" passed, with the extinction of the Counts of Tripoli, to the Kings of Cyprus, and was sometimes granted as a dignity to junior members of the royal house.

The Kingdom of Jerusalem 1099-1187

When Godfrey de Bouillon died in 1100 the crown of Jerusalem passed to Baldwin Count of Edessa. After a short campaign against the Fatimids Baldwin was proclaimed King of Jerusalem on Christmas day 1100. Baldwin was an energetic King who strove to expand the power and territory of the Kingdom. He captured the costal towns of Caesarea and Arsuf from the Saracens in 1101.

The Coronation of Baldwin I "King of Jerusalem" 1100 A.D

In September he again defeated a Fatimid army at Ramalah. It was a glorious victory against the odds. His army of only 250 armoured knights and 1000 infantry defeated Saad el-Dawleh's 10,000 strong Saracen force. The battle was a close run-thing with both sides fighting hard. It was only decided when Baldwin personally led a direct counter attack and routed the Fatimid centre.

In 1102 reinforcements arrived from Europe including Stephen De Blois, the nobleman who had deserted the First Crusade back at the siege of Antioch. At the second battle of Ramlah Baldwin overreached himself. The Crusaders were overconfident and decided to give battle not knowing the strength of the enemy. Unable to escape they had no choice but to launch a direct cavalry charge at the Fatimids. Baldwin managed to escape with a few knights

Seal of Stephen De Blois

to a fortified tower but the remainder of the army was wiped out including Stephen de Blois. Baldwin was ferried out of Ramalah by an English pirate Godric of Finchale who took him to Jaffa. There he raised another army with the help of newly arrived German and French Crusaders and defeated the Fatimids at the battle in Jaffa. During the next few years he continued the struggle against the Saracens and by 1109 the Crusaders captured Tripoli and established the last great Crusader state in the Outremer (Middle East).

The crisis came in 1113 when Baldwin faced a combined assault from the Saracens of Damascus and Mosul. At the battle of Al-Sannabra the Crusaders were enticed into attacking the Saracens who used a feinted flight to entrap them. The Crusaders retreated to a nearby hilltop and fortified themselves on it. Norman reinforcements arrived from Antioch and Tripoli and stabilized the situation. The Muslim attack on the Kingdom subsided when infighting broke within their camp and their leader Mawdud was assassinated.

A great period of castle building commenced during the reign of Baldwin I. In 1115 he built the castle of Montreal (Mont Royal) in the south of the Kingdom.

Montreal castle (Jordan) built by King Baldwin 1115

The Military Orders

In the wake of the First Crusade the Kingdom's Holy Military Orders were created. Hughes de Payens and Godfrey de Saint Omer founded the Knights Templar in 1118. They set up the monastic order on the ruins of the Temple of Solomon in Jerusalem. The other great Military order was the Knights Hospitallers. They originally looked after the sick and

Arms of the Knights Templar

pilgrims visiting Jerusalem, but after the First Crusade they became the defenders of the Holy land.

These Orders grew in power and became the standing army of the Kingdom of Jerusalem in times of trouble.

Bernard de Clairvaux of them wrote;

"A Templar Knight is truly a fearless warrior, and secure on every side, for his soul is protected by the armour of faith, just as his body is protected by the armour of steel. He is thus doubly armed, and need fear either demons or men."

Arms of the Knights Hospitaller

Baldwin II

King Baldwin I died a broken man in 1118, he was forced to repudiate his wife Adelaide (The mother of the Norman King Roger II of Sicily). The crown passed to his cousin Baldwin de Bourcq. Most of his reign would be spent defending the precarious Crusader states from invasion.

The King was captured while defending the frontier of Edessa in 1123. Eustace Grenier was elected Constable of Jerusalem during the King's captivity. He defeated the Fatimid invasion of the Kingdom in 1123 at the battle of Yibneh. The legendry Crusader cavalry charge broke the spirit and will of the Sudanese infantry.

Fulcher of Chartres said;

"The battle did not last long because when our foes saw our armed men advance in excellent order against them their horsemen immediately took flight as if completely bewitched, they went into a panic instead of using good sense. Their foot-soldiers were massacred."

In 1124 King Baldwin II escaped from his imprisonment and returned to Jerusalem. The Crusaders also captured the important coastal city of Tyre establishing a colony and trading links with the new sea power of Venice.

King Baldwin II

Baldwin took the offensive against the Seljuk Turks laying Siege to Aleppo in 1125 and although the siege was broken off after three months Baldwin defeated the Turks at the Battle of Azaz. The King tried to capture Damascus in the following year but again the Crusader forces were not strong enough to finish the campaign. The King died in August 1131 after a reign of over 13 years of non stop-fighting.

A period of instability struck the Kingdom after the death of Baldwin II. By 1132 the Crusaders were fighting themselves. Fulk Count of Anjou reigned as co-consort. He was the Grandfather of Henry Plantagenet, Future King of England and Duke of Normandy. By the 1144 the Kingdom was on the verge of total collapse. Fulk had died and the Kingdom was in the hands of a boy (Baldwin III). Worse still the Crusader State of Edessa fell to the Saracens which send a shockwave back towards Western Europe and led to the Second Crusade.

The Second Crusade 1145-1149

The call to arms did not fall upon deaf ears in the west. Louis VII King of France and Conrad III the German Emperor pledged their support. The two monarchs arrived in the Holy Land in 1147. Instead of attacking Aleppo, which if captured would have allowed them to re-take the County of Edessa, they decided to attack Damascus. The ill conceived strategy proved disastrous. The Crusaders laid siege to Damascus in the summer of 1148, but under constant attack from the Saracens and no real plan of action the Crusade started to fall apart. The Crusaders fought

The Three Kings Baldwin, Louis and Conrad III
The Second Crusade 1148

a desperate battle in the orchards outside Damascus. Conrad the German Emperor led a cavalry charge and had to continue to fight on foot. The Crusaders could not manoeuvre their heavy cavalry in the orchards and decided to move camp. With three Kings but no one in supreme command the Crusade was destined to failure. After four days the different Crusader contingents retreated back towards Jerusalem. The Second Crusade was a missed opportunity to bolster up the defence of the Kingdom and achieve a memorable victory. Blamed on sin, it only made the First Crusade seem even more miraculous. Conrad III returned home to Germany while Louis stayed in Jerusalem for another year until his marriage with Eleanor D'Aquitaine broke down.

The Battle of Ascalon 1153

The Saracen Fortress of Ascalon had been a thorn in the side of the Crusaders for over 50 years. In May 1153 King Baldwin besieged the city. The siege dragged on for four months. In August after heavy bombardment and mining part of the wall tumbled down. At once Bernard De Tremelay (Grand Master of the Templars) stormed through the breach into the city. However he and his knights were surrounded and killed. Their heads were cut off and displayed on the city gates. The Saracens were ecstatic, but their joy was short lived when the Crusaders finally stormed the city on the 19th of August.

Although Baldwin ruled well, the dynastic struggles between the Crusaders nobles undermined the strength of the Kingdom. Rumors circulated that the King had been poisoned from conspirators within the court.

The rise of a united Muslim World

The debacle of the Second Crusade gave rise to the Zengid Dynasty. The Zegrid Muslim Turks began to unite the Muslim world under leadership of Nur ad-Din. He united the former County of Edessa with Mosul, then Aleppo and Damascus in 1154. His power was checked by King Baldwin whom he had a mutual respect for.

When Baldwin III died William de Tyre reported that Nur ad Din Said;

"We should sympathize with their grief and in their pity, spare them, because they have lost a King such as the rest of the world does not possess today."

The new King of Jerusalem Amalric I started his reign well. He formed an alliance with the Byzantines and at the Battle of Al-Buqaia defeated Nur ad Din. Overconfident he invaded Egypt in 1164. This left the Kingdom open to attack from Nur ad Din who had recovered from his previous defeat. In 1164 he crushed the combined Crusader and Byzantine army at the battle of Harim. The defeat was a severe blow for the Crusaders. Some of the leading barons in the Kingdom had been captured, Raymond III of Tripoli, Joscelin III of Edessa, Bohemond III of Antioch and Hugh de Lusignan. Amalric rushed back from Egypt to stop a complete collapse of the Crusader states. The next few years were filled with constant warfare. In 1169 a nephew of one of Nur al Din's commanders became Sultan of Egypt. The mans name would become world renowned in time, for he was Saladin "The champion of the Islamic world"

Saladin and the Leper King

Amalric I died in 1174 and his 13 year old son Baldwin IV became King (commonly known as Baldwin the leper). Saladin's power continued to grow during the 1170s and Baldwin IV had to use all the virtues of Kingship to stop the destruction of the Kingdom.

Success came in the winter in 1177 when Saladin invaded the Kingdom. King Baldwin along with Raynald of Châtillon, Odo De Saint Amand (Grand master of the Knights Templar) Joscelin III of Edessa and the Ibelin brothers headed for Ascalon to garrison the city. Saladin bypassed the fortress and sent a small force to besiege it while he continued his march on Jerusalem.

The Young King Baldwin IV showing the signs of Leprosy

The Battle of Montgisard 1177

The Saracen force that had been sent to hold up the King in Ascalon was by no means strong enough for the task. The Crusaders broke out from the siege and began to gather their forces. Saladin who was unaware of the movements behind him carelessly divided his forces, terrorising the local countryside. Near Montgisard Baldwin's army caught Saladin completely off guard. The King who was quite ill had the relic of the True Cross paraded in front of his knights to encourage them. With no more time to lose the Crusaders unleashed their heavy armoured knights against the unprepared Saracens. The Knight himself led the charge hacking down the Saracen soldiers in his way. He was within inches of killing Saladin who was only saved by nightfall and the bravery of his

Mamluk guards. The Saracen army was wiped and the Kingdom was saved for the time being.

A truce was agreed between the King and Saladin in 1180. It was broken by Raynald of Châtillon who attacked trader caravans passing through his fief on countless occasions.

The Gigantic Crusader castle of "Le Krak des Chevaliers" Syria

The End of the Kingdom

Baldwin's leprosy affected his health and led to his early death in 1185. He had been co-ruling the Kingdom with his nephew Baldwin V since 1183 but the real power in the Kingdom now lay with the leading Barons. When he died, his mother Sibylla and her husband Guy de Lusignan took up the reigns of power.

The Battle of Hattin and the fall of Jerusalem

With Jerusalem weak and fractioned Saladin decided the time was right for the destruction of the Kingdom.

In May 1187 he crossed the river Jordan with an army of over 40,000 men. His first target was Raymond of Tripoli's castle of Tiberias. Guy was now forced into mobilising the army of Jerusalem to combat the invasion.

The fore coming titanic battle would decide the fate of the Holy Land. Guy had two choices, either let the castle fall and defend his current position, or push on to relieve the siege. Foolhardy voices from within the Crusader camp urged Guy to march on and give battle. On the 3rd of July a reluctant King Guy marched off towards Tiberias. They reached the small village of Turan, the last watering spring before Tiberias at midday. With still over eight miles to go the Crusaders marched out in the afternoon, into the barren rocky landscape. As soon as they left Turan Saladin sent his men to capture the village and effectively cut off the Crusaders from any retreat.

With the trap now set Saladin attacked the beleaguered Crusader army as it made its slow progress in the sweltering heat of the summer sun. By evening they were forced to make camp on a plateau that became known as the Horns of Hattin. When the Crusaders awoke on the morning of the 4th of July they found themselves completely surrounded. Their situation deteriorated further when Saladin set fire to the grassland vegetation all around them causing terrible suffering from the heat and the smoke. Raymond of Tripoli despaired;

"God, our war is over! We are all dead men-and the Kingdom has come to an end."

Faced with no alternative but to fight their way out of the trap the Crusaders formed up into battle array. Raymond of Tripoli led the Vanguard, King Guy in the center and Joscelin III of Edessa to the rear. In a desperate attempt to breakout Raymond charged the Saracen lines twice. He managed to breakthrough on the second time, but did not have enough men to counterattack, and with the weight of Saracen number beginning to tell he fled the field. The King was less fortunate. When his knights became separated from the infantry the slaughter began. Vicious hand to hand fighting continued all day until the last remaining Crusaders surrendered.

The Battle of Hattin 1187 (Matthew Paris)

The highly ranking captives were brought to Saladin's royal tent. Saladin offered King Guy water to drink, after a few sips Guy offered the cup to Raynald of Châtillon. Before Raynald could drink it Saladin knocked the cup out of his hands and accused Raynald of being an oath breaker.

Raynald said;

"Kings have always acted thus. I did nothing more."

Saladin had heard enough and with one fatal swoop of his sword he cut Raynald in two. King Guy was shook by the act and fell to his knees expecting the same treatment.

Saladin said to Guy;

"Have no fear. It is not the custom of Kings to kill Kings."

The battle was a total victory for the Saracens. The Crusader field army had been smashed which left the Kingdom virtually defenceless. By late summer he had taken Jaffa, Acre, Nablus, Sidon, Beirut and Ascalon.

In September 1187 his army began the siege of the greatest prize of all Jerusalem. After a futile defence of the city by Queen Sibylla and Balian De Ibelin the city surrendered on the 2nd of October. Saladin was magnanimous in victory. He allowed pilgrims to visit the Holy city and even allowed the Church of the Holy Sepulchre to remain Christian.

Richard the Lionheart against Saladin

The Kingdom of Heaven would live on until its final defeat at Acre in 1291, but the shockwaves of the Saracen capture of Jerusalem would lead to the coming of the Normans again. The Third Crusade was spearheaded by another titanic Anglo-Norman Warrior: Richard the Lionheart, Duke of Normandy and King of England.

Other titles in the series

Richard the Lionheart "THE LAST WAR"

"THE FIRST MAFIA"
The Norman Conquest of Southern Italy and Sicily

"DOMESDAY 1066"
The Norman Conquest and Destruction of
Anglo - Saxon England

"INTO THE DRAGONS LAIR"
The Norman Conquest of Wales and the Marches

Printed in Great Britain
by Amazon.co.uk, Ltd.,
Marston Gate.